# Masterin

# Forex Trading

# Psychology

-The Guide to Mastering the Psychology Behind
Trading the Forex Markets

# Disclaimer

Please not that the information contained within this eBook is for educational purposes only. Every attempt has been made to provide accurate, up to date and reliable information. Please consult a licensed professional before attempting any techniques outlined in the eBook.

By reading this eBook, the reader agrees that under no circumstances is the author responsible for any losses, direct or indirect, which are incurred as a result of the use of information contained within this eBook, including, but not limited to errors, omissions, or inaccuracies.

# Contents

# WHAT IS TRADING PSYCHOLOGY?

Psychology is the study of behaviour and mind, embracing all aspects of human experience. It is an academic discipline and an applied science that seeks to understand individuals and groups by establishing general principles and researching specific cases. This is exactly what we are going to discuss. We are going to use science to show you what's real and what's imagined.

We will dive deeper into the way you think and reveal things about you that you probably didn't even know. We want to discover not only what is really holding you back, but what can pull you forward and make you a profitable trader. Chances are, at this moment, you are not a profitable trader–and if you are, then you think you're leaving money on the table or you wouldn't be here.

What makes trading psychology so important to all traders? Let's start with something simple. Answer this simple question for me: "How much time do you spend working on your mental strategy?"

If you're being honest with yourself, most of you should be right around 0%. If you're compensating and trying to convince yourself that you really do care about the mental component of trading, then you probably came in around 20%-30%. Finally, if you really understand the importance of developing a sound mental strategy, then hopefully you're spending more than 50% of your time dealing with the issues that impact your trading.

"Much learning does not teach understanding." -Heraclitus

This quote demonstrates that no matter how much you think you know, that knowledge doesn't always translate into results. You probably spend 95% of your time trying to perfect or to find the best trading strategy, and you most likely do not even consider how your mental state affects the trading strategy you're using. Your trading strategy could be the best one in history but your inability to execute it is actually what's holding you back.

Professional golfer Raymond Floyd used to boast that he could beat an average golfer if they were to swap swings because he knew how to get the most out of his game. This same phenomenon would happen in trading. If a professional trader took your trading strategy and you took theirs, they would still make more money than you. Why? Because they know how to think their way through the market and to get the most out of each position.

So the choice is yours. You can choose to take the traditional path where you trade recklessly, lose money, and blame it all on your trading strategy. Or you can understand that trading is more about mental toughness than anything else. I am going to introduce you to a different side of trading in which I will not teach trading strategies. Rather, I will introduce you to all those angels and demons inside your mind that are making your decisions. Together, we will help you take control of your trading and become a market wizards.

# WHY ARE YOU TRADING?

Before we even touch the surface of trading psychology, I want you to mentally prepare yourself to answer some tough questions about who you are. I am not here to make you feel better about yourself, or to give you that warm feeling on the inside that everything is going to be okay. Instead, I will encourage you to be introspective and to provide you with the tools of success.

Why are you trading? This is an easy question that most will gloss over. Men like to show their bravado here with an answer like: "To make bank, bro!" But is that the true reason you have taken up trading? Remember, there is no wrong answer here. It could be for a variety of reasons. First, it could actually be to make money. Now I know all of you have the dream of becoming overnight millionaires–but how much money are you hoping to make? Is your goal to become rich? How about to save for retirement? Or maybe you just want to have some fun money? Money is obviously going to be the primary driver for most of you.

One thing that is commonly found amongst the best traders is their desire to be challenged. You could poll many great traders, and they will tell you the money is great; however, what really keeps them coming back is the constant challenge. Trading provides an ever-changing environment that keeps the best of the best on their toes at all times. Great traders love the pursuit of winning–not just once but over the long haul.

Maybe you've decided to become a trader because doing so will give your life purpose. This is a perfectly acceptable answer. We all need goals to pursue. Most people use their jobs as a purpose for living. Luckily for you, trading is the best job in the world.

No matter what it is, it's your reason for being here, so own it. There is no wrong reason to be here. If you want to be filthy rich, then let's make that happen. If you want to turn $20 into

$20 million, then even though that's an honest answer, it's probably not a realistic one.

The more detailed you are, the better off you will be. For example, if you say "I want to be rich," you should delve deeper into that train of thought. Why do you want to be rich? Is it for the status, the nice things you can buy, the people you can help out, or the security that comes with being rich? All of these are fine reasons, but you need to figure this out for yourself.

## CAN MY REASONS CHANGE?

The person you are today will not be the same person you are tomorrow, let alone in five years from now. When you were young, you probably didn't want to be in the profession you are in now. You wanted to be an astronaut or an athlete. However, as time went on, you most likely changed your outlook and thus changed your career path.

The same goes for trading. The reason you began trading will almost certainly change over time. For example, when you started trading you wanted to be filthy rich. As you progress through your trading career, that reason could change to wanting to make money to support your family or to put your children through college. These altruistic considerations often trump the desire to live the life of the rich and famous.

With that being said, I hope you do get so rich that you don't know what to do with all the money you have. I hope you have ten houses and fifty cars, some of which you never use because you have so many of them. In order to get to this point, you're going to have to be willing to be humble, honest, and willing to change or grow.

# WHY DO AMATEURS LOSE?

This is a common question and quite frankly an easy one to answer. Instead of giving you the answer, let's take a little test. Please use a 1-to-10 scale for the following questions:

o Rate your overall trading ability
o Rate your ability to manage your money
o Rate your ability to find good entries
o Rate your ability to get out of bad trades early
o Rate your ability to interpret analysis

Take a few moments to write down your answers. In all likelihood, you gave yourself a so-so score. You probably think you know a decent amount but not know everything. Well, chances are, you're wrong. Chances are you overestimated your skill level and actually gave yourself a better score than you deserved. This is common for everyone and not just you. The phenomenon is called the "Dunning-Kruger Effect."

The Dunning-Kruger effect is a cognitive bias in which people make poor decisions and reach unfounded conclusions. This is due to their incompetence. Unfortunately, this incompetence is what denies them the ability to recognize that they are making mistakes. Furthermore, the fact that the person doesn't recognize their own incompetence causes them to have a superiority complex, causes them to have a superiority complex and believe they possess more skill than they do. The opposite is true for those with superior skills. They tend to underrate their abilities saying they are not as good as they actually are.

The fact is that most of you don't even know enough to realize just how little you know. This is exactly why there is such a high-failure rate in the Forex market. People enter the market, learn very little, and begin trading as if they are professionals. They possess less than 10% of the requisite knowledge, but trade like they have 100%. In contrast, professionals are highly skilled and realize the limits of their own knowledge.

In 1999, David Dunning and Justin Kruger were inspired by the case of McArthur Wheeler. The case was about a man who robbed two banks with lemon juice on his face. The robber had the belief that if he put lemon juice on his face it would act as an invisible ink and thus prevent his face from being recorded on surveillance cameras. After seeing this case, the two men wanted to test if this false sense carried over to other aspects of life.

They proposed that no matter what the skill is, incompetent people fail to recognize their own lack of skill. Dunning and Kruger found this lack of recognition also applies to the estimation of other people's skills. Only when these people are exposed to the proper training and skills of others do they finally recognize their own lack of skill. A perfect example of this is the guy that walks around thinking he can beat anyone in a fight until he actually gets in a fight and gets beat up himself.

The question has to be posed now: How do you cure this so-called syndrome? Well, there are many things that can help. First, admit where you really are at. Understand that if you are new, then your knowledge level is probably a 1 or 2. But that's ok. It's ok to be new and not know much. Start learning now. The next thing you need to do is to track your trades and analyze. We will cover this in detail later on—but analyzing every trade is a must. Finally, the only real cure is financial literacy. You have to educate yourself in this area. It's not going to be glamorous, and it will probably be boring, but it's the only route. I've never met a successful trader who hasn't put in the time and effort to understand the markets.

# RECORD KEEPING

One of the most important things when it comes to trading is keeping a detailed record of your trades. There are many reasons for this, from both a psychological and a data analysis standpoint. Consider this scenario: You have been using the same broker for years, and uncritically assume they are filling your orders at your desired entry point. Little did you know that because you are using market orders, you are experiencing a small amount of slippage on each entry. Until you started keeping records, you had no idea that you in fact are experiencing slippage. Believe me, this small amount of slippage will eventually add up to a large amount of money. The fact that you have kept your own records will allow you to see a glaring weakness in your trading. One that is easily fixed with limit orders.

From a psychological standpoint, we use record keeping to find trends and spot similarities in our winning trades and our losing trades. Each and every one of us has a weakness, and it will rear its head over and over again. The good thing is that we are able to recognize this and to find the remedy for it.

When it comes to keeping a detailed record of our trades, what should we include?

- o • Opening date
- o • Closing date
- o • Security
- o • Direction
- o • Entry
- o • Stop
- o • Targets
- o • Profit/loss

- o ● Risk/reward
- o ● Slippage
- o ● Comments

Each one of these categories will provide insight into our trading tendencies in order to find our strengths and weaknesses. For example, after 1000 trades, you may begin to realize that you win 75% on the EUR/USD pair, but win only 30% of trades on the GBP/USD pair. This is a major red flag. It is something you may have not realized without detailed records. In this scenario, you would need to drill down to the root of the problem and determine if it's even worth your time to focus on the GBP/USD anymore. You may be better off focusing all of your attention on just one pair.

That's the tough thing about trading. We want to trade as many pairs as possible to maximize our profits; however, not all currency pairs are created equal, and some pairs could actually be costing you more money.

## JOURNALING

Journaling is a lost art. We are just so busy with our lives that we don't have five minutes to dedicate to a journal anymore. However, making time to keep a journal can only benefit your trading. Many of the most famous and successful people have kept journals. Some of them include John D. Rockefeller,George Patton,Ben Franklin, Thomas Edison, John Adams, Ronald Reagan, Winston Churchill, Mark Twain, Ernest Hemingway.

However, in today's society, journaling is not popular and often looked upon as something only teenage girls do. My simple question for you is: If these highly successful people kept journals, then why aren't you? For the guys who think journaling isn't manly, I can tell you General George Patton is about as manly as it gets.

Being able to record your thoughts in a journal is one of the best and quickest ways to improve yourself. It is a window into your thought process that allows you to self analyze.

It is no secret that trading is one of the loneliest professions. Chances are, you are sitting behind a computer screen, alone, for hours on end. Even if it's not your main source of income, it is still a lonely endeavor. This is why we tend to gravitate towards message boards and such, just to get a little interaction. Unfortunately, from that loneliness stems hidden and repressed emotions. We often go through the day quashing our emotions and continuing to push forth. This method seems like the smart thing to do in order to stay focused, but these emotions build and often lead us into big mistakes.

By journaling your thoughts and actions, you allow yourself to go back and see the mistakes. You allow yourself to vent and to let your emotions go in a way that is private and secure. And once you have all this out in the open, you relieve so much stress and allow your body and mind to operate at peak performance.

As it relates to trading, there are many things your journaling should focus on. First and foremost, you should always address any outside factors that are affecting your trading. These could include troubles in a relationship, health, etc. These factors are often overlooked in their importance to trading when in reality, the outside factors have about as much to do with your performance as anything.

To piggy back upon this, you should keep a rating of your state of mind. Everyday when you journal, just give yourself a rating between 1 and 10 on your state of mind. hen you go back to analyze, you can see how much a bad state of mind actually affects your ability to trade. When your state of mind rating is 6 or below, you may lose 70% of your trades. On the flip side, you could win 80% of your trades when your state of mind is 7 or higher. This is a clear indication that you should stop trading when you are in a bad place mentally.

Here are some suggestions of what to keep in your journal

- o • Outside factors
- o • State of mind rating
- o • Pre-trade thoughts/comments
- o • Post trade thoughts/comments
- o • Any additional thoughts you may have
- o • A picture of the setup for visual feedback

There are two different ways to journal: handwritten and digitally. It is not uncommon to utilize both. For example, keeping a trade journal digitally in which you record a picture of your trade as well as your thoughts and comments, then keeping a daily handwritten journal of which you address bigger picture issues and problems. Combining these two forms of journaling provides you with the most comprehensive approach. If forced to choose one or the other, I would go with the handwritten journal. Our brain makes a better connection to what we are learning when we write things down. Typing doesn't provide the same connection that handwritten notes do.

# UNDERSTANDING WHO YOU ARE

Your personality is your identity. It is the thing that makes you different from everyone on earth. No two personalities are exactly alike–even those of identical twins who have the same DNA. The reason is because we are all a product of our environments, and we interpret our environments in different ways. Many people can have similar personality types, but no two people are going to have the exact same personality in every facet. Which incites the question: Why do traders all try to copy one another's trading strategies. It would be tough for you to copy another trader's strategies because they probably see the market differently than you do. The information they base their decisions upon will likely be seen differently by you and other traders. Sure you can get pretty close to the same strategy, but there will always be trades that the originator of the strategy sees that you don't, and trades that you see that others won't. The only way to remove this would be to automate your strategy–at which point there would be no reason to worry about trading psychology because you would not be doing any manual trading.

So before we go find a strategy, or before we decide if the strategy you are using is the correct one, let's take a short personality test and determine the type of trader you are. Remember, this is an extremely basic personality test and should be used as a learning opportunity. Be honest!

1. Which describes me best?
a. Aggressive
b. Passive
2. When I win a trade I…
a. Brag to others
b. Go to the next trade
3. I would rather…
a. Read a book
b. Play a sport
4. How much time do you dedicate to trading?

a. Less than 4 hours per day

b. More than 4 hours per day

5. When I've been trading for a long time...

a. I get bored

b. Bored? It's never boring

6. I would describe myself as more...

a. Docile

b. Lively

7. Which mistake do you make more?

a. Impulsive trades

b. Failure to pull the trigger

8. 8. My apartment, condo, or house is...

a. Disorganized

b. Organized

9. When I attend gatherings I am...

a. Outgoing

b. Quiet

10. Which describes me best?

a. Beginner Trader

b. Experienced Trader

Scoring Guide

#1 a=2 b=1

#2 a=2 b=1

#3 a=1 b=2

#4 a=2 b=1

#5 a=2 b=1

#6 a=1 b=2

#7 a=2 b=1

#8 a=1 b=2

#9 a=2 b=1

#10 a=1 b=2

If you scored between 17-20, you're best suited to trade lower time frames. You would benefit from a strategy that allows you to trade quickly. Scalping or fast paced strategies best fit your personality.

If you scored between 13-16, you're best suited for the medium time frames. You would benefit from a strategy that allows you take a few trades each day but you don't want pure chaos. Swing trading would be the preferred strategy, which allows you to hold trades from a few hours to a few days.

If you score 12 or lower, then you're best suited for trading higher time frames. You would benefit from a set-and-forget strategy that allows you to take trades that do not need to be managed very often. You would benefit from a long-term approach.

Hopefully this short quiz has helped establish the framework that you can use going forward. I encourage you to reflect on your personality type further in order to best determine the type of trader you are. Failing to trade the right type of system can be catastrophic. Someone who is uncomfortable with a fast-paced environment is sure to fail in a scalping-style strategy, while someone who thrives under high-stress, fast-paced environments will find long-term trading too boring and most likely leave trading all together.

# ADDRESSING STRENGTHS AND WEAKNESSES

As we continue this introspective journey, we have to address the strengths and weaknesses of you as a trader. I am willing to bet that a very small handful of you have never taken the time to think about your strengths and weaknesses as a trader. Most likely, you dove right into the market and just started trading and haven't looked back since. This is true of both profitable and unprofitable traders.

What you failed to realize is how much potential you are missing out on. In your quest to make money quickly, you forgot to think about your sustainability in this profession.

Do you feel you're going to be trading in 20 years? Hint: most of you won't

Do you feel you can just pick up this vocation and become successful without the work?

Do you expect to be successful in less than a year?

These are all questions you have to ask yourself; however, I can promise you that if you fail to address your strengths and weaknesses, then you won't be around in twenty years. You won't be around in one year!

Addressing weaknesses is essential to being a good trader. Here is an inventory of common weaknesses that prevent good trading practices...

**IMPULSIVENESS**. This is very common among new traders. You are trigger happy and just want to trade. You can't wait to make money because every second you wait is another dollar you're missing out on.

**LACK OF A TRADING PLAN**. If I asked you what your trading plan was, could you explain it explicitly? I hope you'd say "yes." If you did say yes, then I would grill you on every situation. Now, if there are situations when you don't know what you'd do, then there is ambiguity in your strategy.

Instead, you need to define everything about that strategy. Know when you will enter and exit, and most importantly, why you are entering and exiting.

**PROJECTION**. This is when we allow past experiences to negatively impact our current and future trades. If we lose consecutively, then we might be scared to pull the trigger on the next trade. Conversely, if we win a bunch in a row then you may take too many trades because you have this overconfidence about you. This changes your outlook unnecessarily.

These are just a few examples of weaknesses that can easily be addressed and fixed. However, an unwillingness to accept that we have weaknesses is a stumbling block to progress. Often, newer traders are the most vocal of all traders. It seems that once they acquire a little knowledge, and a small taste of success, which could be a few wins, they become vocal about what others do and do not know. This goes back to the Dunning-Kruger effect, according to which novice traders do not know the amount of information and experience they lack until it's too late. These are the same types of people that refuse to admit their weaknesses. To become a great trader, you have to humble yourself enough to realize your flaws. It is only then that you're in a position to begin to improve them.

While weaknesses are often addressed by traders at some point, strengths of the trader are often neglected. It is easy to see why; traders do not address strengths because they do not feel they need to work on them. However, that couldn't be further from the truth. In fact, working on your strengths is something you should be doing on a regular basis. The reason is your strength is what causes you to make money. It is the reason you have an edge in the market. Refusal to improve on it will find you struggling to increase your profits.

Let's take a look at a few examples of some potential strengths:

**TRADE PLAN**. Your trade plan could be so defined that you know exact entries and exits. This is fantastic news because we can use this to refine the plan further. You know exactly where you're missing out on some money.

**DISCIPLINED**. This goes back to your trade plan. You follow your trade plan exactly. This will allow you to see which trades are making you the most money. You'll be able to see what markets you trade the best and what pairs you trade best.

**CALM**. A calm trader is a good trader. This person can trade themselves out of bad situations and stick to the plan. They are able to find triggers that disrupt this calmness and deal with them immediately.

Again, these are just a few examples of strengths that you could be working on. The key to the markets is to find your edge and exploit it. By working on your strengths, you are further sharpening your edge and thus improving your profits.

One of the elements involved in addressing your strengths is the fact that you are establishing goodwill with yourself. This may sound kind of weird at first, but as humans, we naturally remember the bad things in life first while forgetting all the good things. It's as though the bad situations are seared into our minds; however, by acknowledging the good things we do, we are actually relieving stress and building confidence. Sounds strange, I know, but it's a necessary thing—especially in financial markets which have a habit of beating you down.

## THE TRADING PLAN

The trading plan is the one thing each of you has some experience with. Chances are, if you've been trading for some period of time, you have tried more than one trading strategy. But what has stopped you from using certain trading strategies?

Is it because the strategy didn't work?

Is it because you tried to adopt someone else's strategy?

Or is it because you didn't receive immediate gratification so you abandoned it the first sign of trouble?

Now imagine this: Imagine that you stick with one trading strategy forever. You just try to refine it and make it better. Anytime you hit a tough spot, you analyze what is causing the drawdown or consecutive losses, and you fix that. Furthermore, as markets begin to change, you just adapt your strategy moderately to fit the market conditions and keep rolling along.

In this scenario, are you in a better or worse situation than you are now?

I'd be willing to bet that the vast majority of you would be profitable traders in a much better situation. You would have a strategy that was tested, adapted, and implemented by you. You wouldn't be going from strategy to strategy and wasting an enormous amount of time and money skipping around.

So we are going to outline the steps to create your strategy and stress the importance of optimizing one strategy instead of bouncing around to several strategies. We will outline the things you should be considering in your plan, while not getting into the nitty gritty parts of the trading.

Before we talk about the elements you should be considering in your strategy, we need to briefly touch on what style of trader you want to become: a regimented or feel trader.

A **REGIMENTED TRADER** is someone who has a plan that is extremely detailed without any ambiguity. He or she has a checklist of things a setup must meet before entering. The person knows exactly where they will enter, exit, and take profit. Trades are not taken on a hunch or because it is believed a trade will go a certain direction. Rather, trades are taken in a machine like fashion. This type of trading is the surest to remove all emotion.

A **FEEL TRADER**, on the other hand, is someone who has a definite strategy but uses his or her experience and gut feeling to get into trades. This trader's entries, exits, and targets may not be defined, but he or she has a general idea of each one of these elements when entering a trade. Often times these traders like to take a position, then adjust their position throughout after a trade is taken. Emotion is a very real element of this style of trading. To use this style you need to have an exceptional trading mindset that is undeterred by deteriorating situations.

The important thing to note about the style of trader is that there is not a one-size-fits-all method. If you are a freer spirit, you may be better suited for a feel-type strategy. If you are an analytical person, then you may be better suited for the regimented-type strategy. You could have a blend of these two types, but for the most part, if you do not have defined rules that are followed, or if you venture outside of your strategy, then you would be considered a feel trader.

## THINGS TO CONSIDER
## MARKET CONDITIONS

First thing's first: We have to define our market. Market conditions can be split into three groups: ranges, breakouts, and trends—each with a different indication of when the best time to buy or sell might be.

Trading a range strategy in a trending market could have disastrous results. We want to match a range strategy to a ranging market, a trend strategy to a trending market, and a breakout strategy to a breakout market. Now that doesn't mean that you need to trade three different strategies. It is best to start out with one and then adapt that strategy to different types of markets. There are many different tools that can help to determine the volatility and market condition. We will address this in a later lesson.

The most common type of market is the range market. Support and resistance are the main aspects of a range bound strategy. Price is often confined within a channel, with upper and lower limits. A channel may not be perfect looking but identifying the price area where buyer or sellers enter the market is pivotal to effectively trading ranges.

Studies have shown that traders actually trade better in a range-bound market. This is because range-bound markets are typically slower and more predictable. Of course, they're not as sexy as highly volatile or trending markets.

Ranges will eventually break one way or another. This typically happens when fresh news is released that drives the market to breakout. For this reason, if price is at support or resistance levels as fundamental data is released, you should consider not taking the trade and waiting for market conditions that are more predictable.

Obviously, ranges turn into breakouts when price is able to break out of the support or resistance zone. When this happens, traders have received some bit of information that entices them to enter the market and take out previous levels.

I'm sure you've heard it before: "The trend is your friend." The tough part about catching a trend is that the market only trends about 30% of the time. This means that a trend-based strategy should find you doing nothing 70% of the time. The problem that arises is traders don't like to sit on the sidelines and wait, which usually results in losing trades.

Adopting a trend-based strategy can certainly be rewarding. However, you need to take the time and develop a sense of when trends with continue and when they are entering a range or reversal market.

Trading with a bias means that you would only take short trades in a downtrend and long trades in an uptrend. This is to stack the market forces on your side and to give yourself a higher probability of success.

To identify a trend is remarkably easy. Uptrends are defined by higher highs and higher lows. While downtrends are just the opposite, i.e, lower highs and lower lows. This may be a bit confusing at first, but if you spend a short amount of time in front of the charts,you'll quickly find yourself a pro in spotting trends.

After support or resistance is broken, price can continue to run for an extended period of time. Price tends to pick up speed or become more volatile once one of these levels is broken. This is because the market has either gotten fresh news or because the market realizes that the instrument is no longer accurately priced. Looking to enter trades in anticipation of those breaks of support or resistance is trading breakouts.

Trading breakouts can produce more losers than winners. This is due to the uncertainty of when a breakout is actually taking place. Luckily for us, when you're right about a breakout, price can run for an extended period of time which can make up for all the small losses. This is where position sizing and risk reward really make or break the success of this type of strategy. So as you can see trends, ranges, and breakouts can all be interconnected. One can turn into another at any time.

## TREND VS. COUNTERTREND

It is time to discuss what style of trading fits your personality. In many ways, our personality actually shapes our trading plan. Fighting our personality and natural tendencies can have devastating consequences such as the inability to know when to enter and exit trades.

Trend trading is everyone's favorite type of trading because many view it as the safest. This strategy assumes that the present direction of the pair will continue into the future. Trend trading is all about getting into a position and holding it until you believe the trend is done. For this very reason, it is utilized by scalpers all the way up to long term traders.

For example, the trend will change much more often on a fifteen minute chart versus the daily chart. You could have several downtrends on the fifteen minute chart that are contained within the overall uptrend on the daily chart.

With this type of trading you would only be looking to trade with the trend. So, in an uptrend, you would only take long positions, and in a downtrend you would only take short positions. It really doesn't matter what security you're trading– this type of trading would apply to any.

Counter Trend trading is just the opposite. This strategy assumes a current trading trend will reverse and attempts to profit from that reversal. It can be used by short-, intermediate- or long-term traders. Regardless of their chosen time frame, traders will remain in their position until they believe the countertrend move is over.

For example, a fifteen minute chart could be in an overall downtrend. As we all know, trends do not move in a straight line; there are several pullbacks within a much larger trend. The trader would be looking to take advantage of these pullbacks in areas where they feel the pair is overextended or has run out of steam.

## CONSISTENCY

Consistency is the name of the game in trading. It's the thing that will take you from a wannabe trader to one that earns their living from trading. While you may be trying to hit home runs, professional traders are evaluating the market and taking what they can get. They know that by consistently banking a lot of little wins, they can make it add up to a gigantic win.

One thing you should also consider is the simplicity of your strategy. Newer traders often look at simple strategies as losing strategies, but that could not be further from the truth. Simple strategies are easy to follow. They are easy to change. And they are easy to test.

As you find yourself in tough situations—and they will happen more than you think—you want a strategy that's simple and provides specific rules. The more complex and more ambiguous your strategy gets, the tougher it will be for you to remain consistent.

## TESTING

The final and most important aspect of your strategy is verifying it through testing. The testing phase is the perfect time for you to adapt and customize the strategy to fit your psychology. It allows you to see results or pitfalls without actually putting your money in the market. Realize one thing though: Unless you have an automated strategy, your emotional state will be different paper trading versus live-market trading.

There are three different types of testing, and you should make use of all of them. You most definitely will hate testing. It is long, boring, and cumbersome. You will spend countless hours going through each stage that will span weeks, months, if not a year. It is one of those necessary evils of life. Think about it this way: In today's job market, you need a college degree to even be considered for most top jobs. It's one of those things society has acknowledged as a necessity to learn the skills for your desired career path. Going to class is not the most fun thing to do, and it requires a great deal of your time. I know when college is mentioned, many of you automatically revert to late night parties, but if you received your degree then you had to show up for class at some point. Now think about trading. Many of you jump in head first and never study, practice, or do any hard work. And you're wondering why you lose money. So if you're going to trade, get used to testing and learn to embrace it.

The first type of testing is **BACKTESTING**. This is the process of going through historical data and testing your strategy against it. Running a simulation is very easy when you have an automated strategy as there are many different platforms and tools that allow you to run back tests for a defined period of time. However, when it comes to manually backtesting a strategy, things get a little tougher. To manually back test you need to find a trading platform that allows you to use a historical-data feed in market replay mode. Market replay mode allows you to start at an arbitrary date for your specific security and replay the price action to a certain date, which is often present day. This is invaluable for a manual trader as you cannot cheat by knowing what is going to happen. It is like the price swings and fluctuations are happening in real time.

The second type of testing is **FORWARD TESTING**. The name is deceptive but it basically means "to paper trade live markets." This is the phase that takes the longest amount of time. On a back test, you can span months and years of data in a matter of days. Unfortunately, you cannot simulate real time. You have to stick it out and trade the market as you see it. Many traders will find their demons in forward testing. You are exposed to the news and other factors that you may have been able to ignore in back testing.

Finally it becomes time to cut the cord and open a real account but make it extremely small. There is a certain sense of reality that comes with trading actual money. You have no idea what it's like until you actually do it. For this very reason, it is advisable to open small accounts to see how you handle real money situations before putting all your money up.

## WHAT STRESSES YOU OUT?

Stress. Just by saying the word you can feel yourself becoming more stressed out. It is the root of all evil when it comes to trading. Stress is the reason you make bad decisions. Stress is why you felt the need to double your position size to try and make back all your losses. Just think about it. When things are going good and you're winning, you're smiling and joking around and life is good. However, when things are bad and you're in a drawdown, your body tightens up, your brain begins to question what you're doing, and you could find yourself in self-destruct mode.

According to the Mayo Clinic stress can have the following effects on our mind, body, and mood. For example, your body may experience headaches, muscle tension or pain, chest pain, fatigue, change in sex drive, stomach upset, and sleep problems. The problems don't stop there. You could become anxious, irritable, sad, angry, or lack any motivation. This ultimately drives you to have uncontrollable bouts of emotion which sometimes lead to coping mechanisms like alcohol and drugs.

Finding out your stressors has to be one of the first things you do when addressing your trading mindset. A stressor could be something as small as having the TV on while trading or as large as taking a major loss. There will always be things that stress us out; the key is to recognize our stressors and take steps to address and remedy them.

Once we figure out our stressors, the next logical step comes with how do we remove or manage it. If it's an addressable stress, then address it and remove it. If you have CNBC on all day but it annoys you, then turn It off. Heck, turn it off anyway. There's no need to listen to conflicting opinions all day from their experts. Instead, listen to your music of choice. If you have a relationship issue, you better believe that's going to spill over into your work. Fix it now. The only saying is never go to bed angry. For you it should be, never show up to trade angry. It's only going to have negative effects on you and your bank account. Finally, if you can't trade with others around you, then find a private place to work. Turn a spare bedroom into an office or take your laptop in a private place in a local library. There are no excuses for letting stressors get too big.

## RELIEVING STRESS

Relieving your stress will need to be incorporated into your everyday routines. There are many things we do to relieve our stress. For example, you can do physical activity. When you go to see your doctor they always preach the importance of physical activity. Well now it will help you in other ways. You can play sports, go for a walk, or exercise in the gym. Getting up and moving allows you to burn through that stress and reset your mind.

There are many relaxation techniques that you can employ throughout the day if you find yourself getting too stressed. First, take a five-minute break. It is suggested that all people take a five-minute break once an hour while working. This is to refresh our minds. If stress begins to build up, then reach out and talk to someone. Talking through your stress takes it off your shoulders. If you can't find someone to talk to, then begin writing in your journal. You should be keeping a journal anyways, so this is a perfect to put it to good use. Finally, if you can feel that stress creeping into and tightening those shoulders then place a warm towel around your neck and shoulders. This will relax the muscles and help relieve tension.

While relaxation techniques can help you out during the day, meditation can help you prevent stress all together. It can also sharpen your focus and make you a better trader. Meditation is one of the best ways to deal with stress. Research shows it actually helps the brain become resilient to stress. You're training your mind to handle and work through any challenge. Your body learns to deal with stress in a different way and not accumulate it like you did before. Here is a basic meditation technique you can start employing now.

- o • Sit straight up
- o • Feet crossed or on the floor
- o • Deep breaths with eyes closed
- o • Focus on yourself and feel yourself become at peace
- o • Let distracting thoughts pass by like clouds

If you find yourself low on time, then take up yoga. Yoga is an athletic way to help you find a center and relieve stress through activity. It basically combines all the techniques previously stated into one. Now if you think yoga is too easy for physical activity, then just try it. It's a lot harder than it looks. It helps loosen the body up to relieve mental and physical tension.

These are just a short list of the many things you can use to control your stress levels. The fact is that we all experience stress on a daily basis. Some of us are built to handle it better than others, but we can actively take steps to help reduce and relieve the stresses in our life.

Imagine a trading competition that takes place over the course of a year. There are only two traders involved this year, Trader A and Trader B. I guess no one wanted to take on these two traders. Trader A and Trader B have exactly the same strategy, starting capital, technology, broker, etc. The only difference is Trader A addresses his stress levels and has a constant state of low stress. He journals everyday and meditates when he has time. He loves to get away from trading after the day is over and go play basketball with his buddies. Trader B on the other hand does not address stress. He's committed to trading and spends all day and night stressing over every little thing. He is cranky, tired, and worn out all the time. He thinks all this trading psychology mumbo jumbo is for the weak. So who wins the competition? Trader A most likely because his mind is in a much better place, and he will have far fewer mental mistakes. He has allowed himself to step away from trading knowing that it will only benefit him.

No matter if you plan to trade or not, relieving your stress will have positive effects on your life in every aspect.

## THE TRADER'S GRIEVING PROCESS

It's a foregone conclusion that if you trade long enough, you're going to suffer a major loss. You will go through an extended drawdown. You may even blow up your account entirely. The fact of the matter is that trading isn't as easy as it may seem, and it's not all sunshine and roses. Trading is tough and you will most definitely have times of doubt and times of grief. The good news is once you recognize the stages of grief, you can move through them quicker and avoid piling on mistakes.

The stages of grief are fairly universal and can be classified in five or seven stages. For the purpose of this lesson, we have created the five stages of grief a trader goes through. Whether you've already gone through a major loss or will do it in the future, you are likely to recognize the steps.

## DENIAL

The first stage is denial. You don't need to be dealing with a major loss or tough situation to have denial. Denial is most traders best friend. It is the thing that causes many of you to refuse to change or accept the obvious things.

Some of you may take too large of positions and risk too much capital per trade, but if confronted about it you would deny it and find some way to rationalize it. Once you suffer a major loss and are forced to go through the grieving process, your first instinct is to deny that the loss actually happened and that you did anything wrong.

## ANGER

The next phase is anger. As denial begins to wear off, in comes the pain of the actual situation. Denial is great at masking the pain of the situation, but this generally wears off pretty quickly. For a trader, the anger phase is a dangerous one.

Imagine this scenario, you make an ill-advised trade that subsequently ends in a bad loss. After the initial shock, you get steaming mad. You're so mad that you've dedicated yourself to getting it back right now. So you make another trade. This time you double down and… Boom, you lose again. This is a scenario that actually happens a lot more than you might think. When we're angry, it's like we can't see straight let alone think straight.

How thorough do you think your analysis is when you're angry? How likely are you to stick to your trading plan?
Do you think you'd be better off walking away for a little while then coming back?

Anger is one of those involuntary emotions that we battle and struggle with. It gets our adrenaline pumping and leads us to do thing we wouldn't otherwise do. Your anger may be taken out on complete strangers, family, or friends. The only way to really battle it is recognizing when you're dealing with it and take steps to lessen and control it.

Here are a few things you can do to control your anger. Stop. Once you recognize it, stop everything you're doing. Don't finish your sentence or your thought. Stop whatever you're doing at that moment. Breathe. It sounds kind of silly to tell you to breathe, but it's probably something you're not doing in the moment. Take deep breaths and count to ten. This method allows you to pass some time while lowering your blood pressure and adrenaline. Walk away. Probably the best thing to do is walk away. Take a few minutes off. Heck, take the rest of the day off. Too often, anger clouds our judgment, and if we had walked away we would have missed the subsequent bad trades that come from being angry.

The next time you find yourself angry, whether in trading or in life, try these techniques and I promise they will help you out. They can't hurt.

## BARGAINING

After you've gone through those stages of shock and anger where you feel helpless, your natural reaction is to regain control. This is where you begin bargaining with yourself. This is that "if only" stage.

If only I had waited to get…
If only I had moved my stop…
If only I had cut my loss when I wanted to…

All of these 'if onlys' are you attempting to revise the past and take back that feeling of control.Even though you are questioning yourself, you are in control of the questions and feel that you could have controlled the situation.

All in all, this is a weak line of defense that usually doesn't last long from the actual pain that we feel.

## DEPRESSION

Unfortunately, that weak line of defense in which you reason with yourself leads to the inevitable depression. Now depression manifests itself in many forms and severities. You could have a feeling of depression that is gone quickly by simply getting a hug from a loved one and the assurance that everything will be all right. Other forms of depression really embed themselves into our thoughts and actions. You feel lethargic and moody. You can be seen moping around and often feel sorry for yourself. You may let things get to you that you wouldn't otherwise.

For a lot of people this is that "give up" phase. You feel there is no hope in sight, so you give up on what you have been working for.

Many traders fail, but a lot of traders fail because they are not smart with their money and they cannot mentally handle losing. Sometimes these go hand in hand where the trader takes a large loss and can never move past it.

Depression is something everyone feels throughout their life. It's not seen as socially acceptable to talk about it with others. People typically bury it away and think they can move past it, but it's not always that simple. For that reason, it should be permissible for you to discuss your feelings about trading with someone you can trust. Find a psychologist and express your feelings to them. Write down your feelings in a notebook if you think there is nowhere to turn. Just make sure you release whatever is holding you back.

## ACCEPTANCE

Once you release that burden or pain, you can finally enter the acceptance phase. This isn't the phase where everything is all better; it is the phase where you have come to terms with the grief and are able to move forward. Some traders will never be afforded this stage. They cannot get past their denial or anger and never reach any form of acceptance. Just because there are five stages of grief doesn't mean you reach each stage.

The acceptance stage only comes when we allow ourselves to feel grief instead of avoiding it. Avoiding the pain and the process will only prevent you from healing.

### **REMOVING EMOTION**

Trading is much like other businesses where the more certainty, the better. That means that if we can predict what's going to happen in both good times and bad, then we can better prepare ourselves for both situations. The problem with certainty and trading is that, as traders, we know we need something that is safe and predictable but that's not what draws us to the market. It's that level of uncertainty that gets us excited. That feeling of today I could be bankrupt or a millionaire. Even though that's an extreme example, but it's not far off the truth.

As a human being you subconsciously love that level of uncertainty. Why? Because it's fun and exciting. That's what's so exciting about the financial markets. Today will be different than tomorrow, and tomorrow will be different than the next day. Sure you can go in with a plan, but anything can happen and that's what excites people. Now remove that excitement. Every day you will trade the same strategy no matter what happens. Massive market moves will not excite you because you're not trying to chase them. Instead you stick to your plan and trade the same way, day after day. Do you think you might get bored? I'll answer that for you. Yes, you're going to get bored. Some days you may not take a trade. You may have to sit on your hands and watch the charts. Think you could do it? The answer to this question is pivotal.

Professional trading is about following a blueprint and not giving into those urges that could possibly hurt you. That's why many try and fail. Even when they have the winning blueprint, they continue to go after that excitement and uncertainty instead of opting for boring and consistent.

## UNCERTAINTY BREEDS EMOTION

If you're that trader that enjoys uncertainty and claims to have made it work then you still have another hurdle to jump over. Time and time again when a trader can't explain their trading method or why they make trading decisions they claim to be feel traders. This is completely fine but how will you "feel" when you're stuck in a losing position with no real plan. Do you opt to stick it out and wait for it to go in your direction, or do you cut bait now while you still have some money left in your account? My only hope for you is that you have your emotions under control at this moment because clarity is what you'll need.

The more uncertainty we allow in our trading, the more emotion we allow to affect our decisions. Uncertainty is the breeding ground for emotion. When you're in a situation and you cannot predict the outcome, what do you think will show up first: confidence or doubt? For the majority of you, it will be doubt. This is because you have no idea if you're going to suffer a massive loss or if you're going to get out unscathed.

## REMOVING EMOTION

At this stage we have proven that emotions and excitement, while fun, do not generally translate into larger bank accounts. Instead for the vast majority of traders, certainty and boring old trading are the best ways to grow and build an account. So it raises the question, how do we completely remove our emotions?

Well the simple fact is you can't–you're human. Humans are emotional and make bad decisions all the time. The only way to combat this is preparation and practice. Which means the first step you need to take is to define a trading plan. It seems as though we keep circling back to the trading plan because without it, you're doing all this in futility.

Even with all the preparation in the world, you're still going to lose. I don't mean just one trade, I mean a lot of trades. This brings us to acceptance. Might as well accept it right now that you will have losses. You will not only lose one trade but you will lose several trades. You will have down weeks, down months, and potentially down years. I know you're not a hedge fund but the best hedge funds in the world have down weeks, months, and years all the time.

# BILL DUNN

Bill Dunn started Dunn Capital Management in 1974 with nineteen partners. Together they started with $137,000. That's it. This wasn't a billion dollar hedge fund. They had only $137,000. Today that's equivalent to around $700,000. Significantly more but still not exactly what you'd call a major hedge fund. Today he manages more than one billion in assets. Not too shabby wouldn't you say. Let's take a closer look at his performance month by month.

Below you will find Bill Dunn's World Monetary and Agriculture Program stats. It is his most popular program that he offers. He utilizes trend following techniques in the futures market. To even be considered for this program you need an initial investment of 10 million. So if you were thinking of just having Bill Dunn do the work for you, you may need to start saving.

Key stats
Winning months = 55%
Losing months = 45%
Largest losing month = 23.52%
Largest winning month = 31.22%
Average yearly performance = 19.21%
Average Monthly performance = 1.65%
Most consecutive losing months = 5
Most consecutive losing years = 3

So you can see that no matter who you are, you cannot avoid losing. Accept what happens and move forward. If you were to analyze these stats without any frame of reference, you might conclude that this trader was extremely average and you probably wouldn't invest your money with them. That is until you found out that he's averaging nearly 20% a year. That's not 20% with a $100,000 account. That's 20% on a fund worth billions. So let's say that you invested 100 million with Bill Dunn, this time next year you'd have 120 million. Assuming you kept your money with him for another year, your account would swell up to 144 million. You've made 44 million by simply doing nothing and letting Bill Dunn manage your money. Moral of the story is that if you can average decent returns, the money will find you. You don't need to double your account every week or month. Rather focus on the long term and consistently making profits.

## MANAGING EMOTIONS

Even though you think you can remove emotion, chances are you probably cannot. You're human for crying out loud. However, you can learn to manage it and control it. Emotions are what make humans who they are. Managing our emotions are an essential thing though when it comes to trading. The ability to accept what has happened, good or bad, and move forward is essential to being a great trader.

The best strategy you can use is to stop thinking money, and start thinking process. Think more about the steps of your trading plan than the potential outcome. Money complicates everything. You are here to make money but once you start winning or losing it, it automatically complicates things. However, if you stick purely to process, then you're able to find that trading zone faster and avoid a lot of the money complications. Seems much easier to say than actually do and it is, but thinking in terms of process allows you to take a systematic approach and removes a lot of the excess emotions.

## PUTTING IT ALL TOGETHER

This process you have gone through has been an introspective look at your psychology. I hope you have taken the time to digest it all and implemented as much as you feel comfortable with. In the end, you have to take responsibility for your own trading. Do not be the person that blames someone else for bad trades. If you choose to execute a trade then that is your choice, no matter if you are using your own analysis or someone else's.

Printed in Great Britain
by Amazon

59994975R00025